The Power of
POSITIVE AFFIRMATIONS

Each Day a New Beginning

ALEX UWAJEH

The Power of Positive Affirmations: Each Day a New Beginning

The Power of
POSITIVE AFFIRMATIONS

All scripture quotations in this book are from the Holy Bible: New King James Version, King James Version, New International Version, Amplified Version and American Standard Version.

First, let's look at Hebrews 4:12 New King James Version:

For the word of God is living and powerful, and sharper than any two-edged sword, piercing even to the division of soul and spirit, and of joints and marrow, and is a discerner of the thoughts and intents of the heart.

And, Jeremiah 15:16 New International Version simply says:

When your words came, I ate them;
   they were my joy and my heart's delight,
for I bear your name,
   Lord God Almighty.

Now, go to Psalm 119:103, 105 New King James Version:

 How sweet are Your words to my taste,
Sweeter than honey to my mouth!

Your word is a lamp to my feet
And a light to my path.

Let's look at one more thing, **Isaiah 55:11** New King James Version:

So shall My word be that goes forth from My mouth;
It shall not return to Me void,
But it shall accomplish what I please,
And it shall prosper in the thing for which I sent it.

In Psalm 34:10. The Bible says, New King James Version:

The young lions lack and suffer hunger;
But those who seek the Lord shall not lack any good thing.

The Power of
POSITIVE AFFIRMATIONS

CONTENTS

Introduction

Your life really does stem from your thoughts. Your thoughts drive your words, which in turn drive your actions.

Did you know that focusing on the negative aspects of things could actually make more negative things appear in your life?

For example, if you complain about how unwell you are and how badly you feel, chances are you're going to keep feeling bad. Your thoughts keep churning about how awful you feel, so your words reflect those thoughts.

The Power of
POSITIVE AFFIRMATIONS

You might find yourself telling those around you how hopeless a situation is, or why things will never happen, or how bad a particular situation seems. The more you voice those concerns, the more your mind will focus on those things. The result is that you get more of the same negative results in return.

Have you ever found yourself in a conversation with someone who spent the entire time moaning about how bad things are? They complain about even the smallest things and manage to find something negative in every situation. They put themselves and others down, and they make it very clear with their words that

they have very little faith in their own ability to create any type of positive outcome. They may also find plenty of faults in everyone around them, almost as though they're looking for anything negative to nit-pick about.

By the time you've ended your conversation with a negative person, it's likely you feel just as drained and worn down as they do.

Of course, the reverse is also true. Did you know that looking for a positive aspect in any situation could actually make more positive things appear in your life?

Have you ever met someone who was so positive about life in general, even in the face of massive negativity and setbacks? No matter how bad the situation might seem, there are people who will accept those things they can't change and they'll spend their energy looking for the positive side of every event that comes their way.

For example, it may be pouring with rain outside, but a positive person will only see that rain rejuvenates the garden and offers a bit of relief from stifling heat. A person with a positive outlook will view each morning as a new opportunity to generate new sales or learn something new to improve his skills or apply for that dream job or meet the person of their dreams.

At the end of a conversation with a positive person, it's far more likely you'll feel as uplifted and motivated as they do. You're likely to walk away from a conversation with a positive person with a smile on your face. That type of positivity really is contagious!

The key to living a happy, fulfilled and successful life is to learn to adopt a positive outlook. No matter how bad, negative or

difficult a situation might seem on the surface, there is always a positive side somewhere.

Are you ready to change your life?

Chapter One

POSITIVE SELF-AFFIRMATIONS

Affirmations are simply positive statements that can help change your entire outlook on everything in your life. In fact, there is some research showing that affirmations can play an important part in breaking negative thought patterns. By breaking the pattern of negative thought, you also begin breaking the patterns of negative words.

As a result, you should notice that you're able to break the pattern of negative actions. Every word you speak has the power to influence the actions you take.

For example, when you're faced with a challenge, does that little negative voice inside your mind start saying "you can't do that"? The moment your inner voice tells you that you can't do something; your words will reflect those thoughts.

When you think you can't do something, the words you speak will reinforce those thoughts.

☐ "I can't lose weight"

☐ "I can't afford that"

☐ "I can't get a good job"

Whenever you think something negative, your actions will follow suit. As long as you believe something can't be done, your actions will

ensure that your thoughts are correct. You won't keep trying to lose weight. You won't look for ways to cut your spending or boost your income so you can afford the things you want. You may stop trying to apply for jobs that would be more fulfilling.

The result of taking negative action – or no action at all - is that you'll never achieve your goals or dreams.

Yet by learning how to use positive self-affirmations you can change that negative inner voice. Instead of thinking "I can't do that", change that inner negativity and look for a more positive way to approach a challenge or problem.

Most people believe that telling themselves they CAN do it will be enough to change those negative thoughts. However, if you don't really believe you're capable of achieving something, deep down inside yourself, chances are your

words will still not accept even the simplest of positive affirmations.

Instead, try asking yourself "how can I achieve this?"

By asking your sub-conscious mind 'how' you immediately open your mind up to alternative possibilities that you wouldn't have been able to recognize otherwise.

Once you start asking, "How can I achieve this?" your words will start reflecting those inner thoughts. You might start asking the right questions of people who may have the answers you seek. You could start talking to the right people who might offer the direction you're looking for.

You could start researching options that could lead to positive outcomes you might not have considered before. You might even start discussing the problem with a view to finding a

real resolution to whatever challenge you're facing.

It's at that point your thoughts become words. And words have real power!

Your words could open up entire new doors you may never have considered before, leading you to taking positive actions towards achieving your goals.

No matter what challenge you face in your life, take note of those pesky inner voices in your mind. If you catch a negative thought passing through, change it to something more positive.

For example:

> Instead of believing you're not smart enough to learn something new, ask yourself how you might learn more about a particular topic.

Rather than tell yourself that you can't lose weight, ask yourself how you can be healthier and happier each day.

Instead of telling yourself you can't afford the nice things you want in life, ask yourself how you can find a way to afford them more easily.

Don't let your inner voice tell you your relationship is troubled. Ask yourself what would make your relationship happier and more harmonious instead.

If you're single, don't let your inner voice tell you that you're somehow unworthy of a loving relationship. Instead, use positive affirmations to remind yourself that somewhere out there the perfect partner is

out there looking for someone exactly like you – and that perfect partner is getting closer with each passing day.

When your inner voice tells you it's Monday morning and you hate your job, turn that into a positive affirmation instead. Tell yourself it's the beginning of a bright new week and you're going to make a real difference in your job role.

Instead of thinking you'll never find a job, change that inner thought. Tell yourself you're another day closer to finding the right job that will pay you properly for your time and efforts.

Don't let your inner voice tell you that you're not attractive enough or you're

somehow unworthy. Change those negative thoughts and remind yourself that you are unique. Nobody else has your sense of humor, your charm, your wit, your intelligence or your knowledge. Those things are unique to you and they make you special.

No matter what challenge or obstacle you're facing, your inner thoughts will dictate the words you use and the actions you take.

Take notice of the things you tell yourself inside your mind. Listen to those negative thoughts. Look for ways you can be more positive about whatever situation you're facing.

Chapter Two

BUILD YOUR FAITH

Far too many people have very little faith in their own abilities. The number of truly talented, unique, wonderful people out there who don't believe they're capable of achieving success is staggering.

In fact, no matter what aspect of life you consider, there are deserving people out there who just can't seem to catch a break. When you talk to those people, their words sound like they are already defeated.

They will tell you they've tried everything, but nothing ever works. They'll say they're always sick, or not attractive enough, or not smart enough to achieve their dreams. They'll say they

must be living with a secret curse, or that they're just not lucky enough to catch the big breaks, or that they're not smart enough to find a way out of their predicament.

All of those words are negative, and they stem from the spiral of negative thoughts inside their own minds. Those thoughts turn into the negative words they say to the people around them, which simply reinforces their own belief that nothing will ever go right for them.

Now think about those people who seem to cruise through every situation and challenge before them as though nothing can stop them. Everyone knows a successful person who just seemed to be in the right place at the right time. We all know someone who is in a happy, loving relationship with the ideal partner. And there are always people out there who seem to just be lucky enough to have all those big breaks land right in their laps.

If you stop and listen to the words those 'lucky' people say, you might notice a big difference between those people and the unfortunate people who just can't make things go their way.

Chances are the words those seemingly lucky people use are almost always positive. Their positive inner thoughts have helped them develop a strong belief that they should achieve success in their endeavors.

Their minds are already in a state of believing that opportunities will arise. This leads them to speak more positive words to others that reflect their belief in their own ability.

Of course, when an opportunity does present itself they'll be ready to take action and seize it when it arrives.

The same principle is true for any goal you want to achieve.

If you want your business idea to succeed, you first need to believe it's possible.

If you're seeking a happy relationship, it's important that you first believe that the right person for you is on the way.

If you're searching for a new job or a change of career, you really need to believe you deserve the opportunity that's coming your way.

If you want to enjoy good health, you first need to believe that you can enjoy living a healthy lifestyle.

If you want a more active social life, you need to believe there are lots of people out there who will truly cherish you for being uniquely you.

If you want to earn more money in your career, you'll have to believe you're worthy of the extra pay before it starts to arrive.

The only way to achieve those things is to build your faith by developing a more positive attitude. Trust yourself and God given abilities. Be brave enough to reach for your goals, even if you only take small steps at a time. With every little step you take, at least you know you're headed in the right direction.

Use positive affirmations to help dispel those negative thoughts. You should notice that your confidence in your abilities starts to improve very quickly.

As your confidence builds, the words you use in conversation will reflect your enthusiasm. Your enthusiasm will spark happier thoughts in your mind, which can uplift you and reduce stress. You'll feel happier in yourself, which is often enough to boost your morale and your motivation.

In turn, others will notice your positive attitude. You'll radiate happiness and enthusiasm, which automatically makes people enjoy your company more. They'll want to learn more about your goals and why you feel so enthused. As a

side benefit, they'll also start to notice they feel happier whenever they associate with you.

Before you know it, you'll have people all around you who genuinely enjoy your company.

Your stress levels will be lower than ever before. You'll be more motivated during your daily tasks. You'll feel positive about yourself and your ambitions, which can lead you to reaching out for new opportunities you might otherwise have missed.

You may even notice your health is improving, because you're focusing on more positive aspects of your life.

Have faith and you'll find it's much easier to achieve your goals and dreams.

Mark 11:22-25 New King James Version says:

So Jesus answered and said to them, "Have faith in God. For assuredly, I say to you, whoever says to this mountain, 'Be removed and be cast into the sea,' and does not doubt in his heart, but believes that those things he says will be done, he will have whatever he says. Therefore I say to you, whatever things you ask when you pray, believe that you receive them, and you will have them.

"And whenever you stand praying, if you have anything against anyone, forgive him, that your Father in heaven may also forgive you your trespasses.

Chapter Three

CHANGE FROM THE INSIDE-OUT

What does the word 'abundance' mean to you? For most people it means being wealthy enough to buy anything your heart desires.

But what if you could live an abundant life without ever having to worry about money ever again? There are many different types of abundance that so many people overlook.

For example, your life could be abundantly happy. It could be filled with abundant love. It could be filled with an abundance of success or pleasure or contentment or knowledge.

Now, what if you believed your entire life could be as abundant as you want it to be?

So many people feel overwhelmed by life that they never really stop to take note of the good things around them. Daily pressures to keep up with deadlines and work schedules and home chores and family obligations usually take up the bulk of our focus.

By the time you go to bed at night, your mind is already focusing on how you're going to get through the same list of chores all over again the next day. The thought of such drudgery can make it really difficult to focus on anything positive. That's usually when people turn inwards and focus on their own emotions.

For instance, have you ever felt down and dejected because you felt as though nothing ever goes right for you? Those negative emotions often lead to a spiral of even more negative emotions.

You might feel down and dejected after a small setback. Those emotions can lead to self-judgment and self-criticism, frustration, and sometimes even jealousy of others. All of those negative feelings can lead to emotions like resentment and anger. In some cases, they can even lead to feelings of anxiety and depression.

When you're caught in a cycle of negative emotions, it's common for many people to turn to various substances to make them feel better. Drugs or alcohol or even binge eating can be very common substances people use to give them a temporary sense of comfort and relief, but they don't actually stop those negative emotions from resurfacing again.

In fact, they can often be a catalyst for even more negative thoughts that can start the cycle all over again. Some people continue to repeat

this vicious cycle over and over again, because they simply don't know how to break it.

So how do you get rid of those negative thoughts and emotions, and break that cycle for good? How can you improve your emotional state so you can live your life abundantly in all the things you want to enjoy in your life?

Whenever you recognize those negative thoughts taking control of your mind, stop and take a moment to ask yourself a simple question:

"Why am I feeling this emotion right now?"

Are you frustrated because you feel powerless to do anything about your situation? Rather than focusing on being unable to do much, switch your thoughts to what you can do positively

instead. Even a small step forward is far more positive than never taking a step at all.

Are you feeling self-critical because you gave in to temptation and ate too many cookies after a bad day? Rather than wallow in the self-loathing and critical self-blame, look for a more positive thought pattern.

Are you beating yourself up for not being good enough to get that job or find that ideal relationship or achieve that goal? Stop focusing on the negative outcomes and take a step back. Look at what caused those bad feelings in the first place.

Then ask yourself why you're feeling the emotions you feel.

Really be honest with your answers! In many cases, the emotions you're feeling could be the result of a spiral of negative thoughts in your mind.

The way you deal with life's situations changes when you start to think more positively.

For example, imagine you've had a bad day and you come home to drown your sorrows. So you eat a whole tub of ice cream. Once the tub is empty, you feel guilty and embarrassed and ashamed. You look in the mirror and hate the person staring back at you, which sparks a whole new cycle of negativity.

These are all emotions and feelings that focus on self-criticism, so they're definitely not positive.

Rather than let your mind continue with a negative train of thought, ask yourself why you're feeling those emotions after a bad day. You may answer that the emotion is because you felt powerless, or because you don't enjoy your job, or because you feel undervalued at

work, or that your partner doesn't value you enough.

When you dig a little deeper, you should start to notice that each of those answers has nothing to do with you. If you're feeling powerless, it's because someone higher up than you has all the power and you have no control over changing the chain of command.

If you don't enjoy your job and you feel burned out by the time you get home, that's also nothing to do with who you are. It's simply that you're working in the wrong position to benefit your future.

If you feel undervalued at work, that emotion is also not aimed directly at who you are. It's aimed at how others perceive your performance at your job description.

The Power of
POSITIVE AFFIRMATIONS

If you're feeling bad that your partner doesn't seem to value all you do for them each day, don't automatically resort to self-criticism. Instead, consider the possibility that your partner's perspective has nothing to do with who you are as a person, but is more based on what their own mind is telling them to look for in other people.

The things that make you feel bad about yourself are not always about YOU.

This is obvious when you sometimes react in a personal manner to the way others cast their negative beliefs towards you.

Instead of punishing yourself for what other people's negative thoughts are casting out, look for ways to see the positive in everything you've done.

The Power of
POSITIVE AFFIRMATIONS

You may have done everything right at work. You may have been the perfect partner. You may be a witty, talented, funny, loving, wonderful person, but if someone else isn't willing to open his or her eyes and see your true value, that certainly isn't your fault.

The only real way to feel the level of confidence required to stop scolding yourself for everything you do wrong is to learn how to control your negative thoughts and replace them with positive affirmations.

When you develop the habit of looking for the positive in every situation, you'll soon find there's no need to blame yourself for the things that go wrong around you. In fact, you'll start seeing everything you do as a new opportunity to learn and grow and improve.

As you begin to form a habit of searching for more positive thoughts to replace those negative emotions, you will notice that your actions start to change at the same time.

The actions you take in response to the events in your life are what will dictate the results you achieve.

Now, boldly declare God's Word:

Psalm 91:1-7 New King James Version:

He who dwells in the secret place of the Most
High
Shall abide under the shadow of the Almighty.
 I will say of the Lord, "He is my refuge and my
fortress;
My God, in Him I will trust."

Surely He shall deliver you from the snare of
the fowler
And from the perilous pestilence.
He shall cover you with His feathers,
And under His wings you shall take refuge;
His truth shall be your shield and buckler.
You shall not be afraid of the terror by night,

Nor of the arrow that flies by day,
Nor of the pestilence that walks in darkness,
Nor of the destruction that lays waste at
noonday.

A thousand may fall at your side,
And ten thousand at your right hand;
But it shall not come near you.

Now, let's take this further:

Look at **Psalm 121,** New King James Version:

I will lift up my eyes to the hills—
From whence comes my help?
My help comes from the Lord,
Who made heaven and earth.

He will not allow your foot to be moved;
He who keeps you will not slumber.
Behold, He who keeps Israel
Shall neither slumber nor sleep.

The Lord is your keeper;
The Lord is your shade at your right hand.
The sun shall not strike you by day,
Nor the moon by night.

The Lord shall preserve you from all evil;
He shall preserve your soul.
The Lord shall preserve your going out and your coming in
From this time forth, and even forevermore.

Now, read **Joel 2:25** King James Version:

And I will restore to you the years that the locust hath eaten, the cankerworm, and the caterpiller, and the palmerworm, my great army which I sent among you.

Chapter Four

TURNING POSITIVE THOUGHTS AND POSITIVE ACTIONS INTO QUALITY LIVING

Everyone has amazing daydreams. You know the ones: you land your ultimate job or you finally meet that ideal partner. Your daydreams might feature a stunning mansion or a flashy sports car or a wildly successful business.

Your daydreams might be awesome, but do you really believe deep down inside you that they'll ever come true?

Most people don't.

Those daydreams are nothing more than fantasies we love to indulge in to escape from some aspect of our lives we're not happy with. And they're perfectly normal.

However, what if you could turn your thoughts into positive actions that could help you make some of those dreams turn into reality?

When you verbally affirm your dreams, goals and ambitions, you're instantly empowered with a deeper sense of reassurance that your words might become reality.

As you reinforce those positive words, you'll find that your actions start reflecting that sense of reassurance you've developed. You may only take small steps towards attaining your desires, but those baby steps are still headed in the right direction.

The Power of
POSITIVE AFFIRMATIONS

The more you work on dispelling those negative thoughts and replacing them with more positive affirmations, you'll start to believe you really can achieve your goals. You'll experience an automatic increase in confidence that gives you the courage to reach even further towards reaching your destination.

Create a list of positive affirmations that work for you and your goals. Keep them somewhere you can read them regularly and say them aloud whenever you get the chance.

The more you repeat your affirmations, the more you'll believe they're possible for you. As you speak your affirmations out loud, your mind will start to look for alternative solutions to making them into your reality.

It all begins with changing your thoughts.

Chapter Five

NEW BEGINNING AND A FRESH START

Look at Isaiah 43:19 New King James Version:

Behold, I will do a new thing,
Now it shall spring forth;
Shall you not know it?
I will even make a road in the wilderness
And rivers in the desert.

No matter how bad things seemed yesterday, today is a brand new beginning. Each new day

is a new opportunity to reach a little further towards your destiny.

One of the key factors in how your day progress is the attitude in which you start your day.

Have you ever looked in the mirror and thought, "*I look terrible*"?

Whatever your mind focuses on, your actions will try to turn into reality. If you believe you look terrible, your mind will reinforce that belief. Your thoughts influence your actions.

The result of those actions is that you feel terrible. Your thoughts determined your actions, which turned into a self-fulfilling prophecy. The next time you look in the mirror, your mind will repeat the negative thoughts again because it now believes it to be true.

The Power of
POSITIVE AFFIRMATIONS

Think about this: when you focus on all the things your partner does wrong, chances are you'll always find something to criticize.

But what if you look for what your significant other is doing right instead of focusing on the negatives? When you start looking for all the things your partner is doing right, you'll start to notice that even those seemingly 'wrong' things are sometimes positive actions in disguise.

For example: you might book a romantic dinner for the two of you at a fancy restaurant, but your partner arrives 20 minutes later than you planned to meet. While you're sitting there alone, do you get frustrated and angry that your partner was too inconsiderate to arrive on time? Do you start thinking your partner has no respect for you or your relationship and start questioning your future together?

All of those negative emotions are based on the unknown. You have no idea why your partner is late until they arrive at the restaurant.

How would you feel if your partner was late to dinner because he stopped off at the store to buy you a gift on the way? What about if your partner got caught in a car accident on the way?

Those incidents have nothing to do with all the negative emotions you might have been feeling. In fact, if you'd been sitting at that restaurant thinking about all the things your partner does right, chances are you would have been sitting at the table with a happy smile on your face when he or she finally did arrive.

Have you even stopped to think about what emotions your partner might be feeling while they're running late for your meeting? Are they feeling anxious, nervous, worried or frustrated?

Each of those negative feelings revolves around fear of how you might react when your partner finally does arrive at dinner later than expected. In this example, you're both feeling negative, but for very different reasons. Unfortunately, the result of all that negativity is often an argument.

By comparison, truly happy couples accentuate the positive things in life. It's really all about perspective.

The same principle is true for almost every situation in your life. You can translate the same circumstances to your work place or your social life. Focus on the things people do right, not what they're doing wrong.

If you find that some of your friends, colleagues or associates are just negative people, make the choice to move on. After all, when your friends all have negative attitudes it can be easy to fall into the same patterns.

The Power of
POSITIVE AFFIRMATIONS

You all start looking for the bad in everything and everyone. You might start talking about all the horrible things that have happened to you. You may even start focusing on how nothing good ever happens.

Then you are left feeling deflated and negative about the world.

However, when you make the decision to avoid associating with negative people your own attitude will start to change for the better.

Find ways to associate with more positive people. You'll find that positive people are usually happy. Happiness is often contagious, so you'll feel good when you're around them.

Positive people are also enthusiastic about their dreams and goals. It can be a great way to build your own self-confidence and moral as you

listen to them recount the little steps they take towards achieving their desires.

What's more, positive people often look for the bright side in every situation. No matter how bad you might feel about a situation, hanging out with positive friends can be a great way to start looking for a bright side that just might become a solution to your issue.

Make a fresh start on your attitude. Think about ways to improve your own inner thoughts. Take action on those thoughts and use that motivation to increase your circle of friends and colleagues to include more positive people.

Chapter Six

SHOW YOUR GRATITUDE

1Thessalonians 5:18 says, "In every thing give thanks for this is the will of God in Christ Jesus concerning you" Thank you Father for strength as I wait on you.

Psalm 150:6 New King James Version simply says:

Let everything that has breath praise the Lord.

The Power of
POSITIVE AFFIRMATIONS

So many people complain about all the things they don't have. Yet, how many times do you hear people say they're grateful for the things they already have?

Being grateful for the things you already have in your life can be a wonderful way to bring out the positive attitude in almost everyone.

When you learn to be grateful for even the small things in your life, your troubles don't seem so overwhelming. It's also a great way to recognize that life might not be nearly as bad as your negative thoughts might want you to believe.

Take a few moments to look for things in your life that you're truly grateful for. You can be grateful for the sunshine and the rainfall or where you are at this point in time. You can be grateful you've had opportunities that so many people in the world might never experience.

The Power of
POSITIVE AFFIRMATIONS

It's surprising how many people believe they have nothing at all to be grateful for. Yet when you look a little more deeply, you'll be surprised at just how much gratitude you can find in even the simplest things in life.

Do you hate the bitter cold of winter? Be grateful that you can find ways to stay warm when so many people can't.

Do you feel sad when it rains? Be grateful that the rain is nourishing your gardens.

Do you dislike your job? Be grateful that you have a source of income when so many people don't.

Have you lost your job? Are you struggling to get another job? Give thanks for what you have lost and believe God for a better one or a new career path.

Do you feel like a failure? Be grateful that you had the opportunity to give it a shot in the first place. You also have the opportunity to learn what might have gone wrong so you won't repeat those same actions in future.

Do you always feel as though you never have enough money? Money can't make you happy anyway. There are rich people out there who are miserably unhappy, so be grateful you have your health and your happiness.

Are you disillusioned by your relationship? Be grateful that someone out there saw something special in you.

Did your partner leave you and now you're single? Be grateful that you still have the opportunity to meet the right person to spend your future with when the time is right.

It makes no difference what aspect of your life you consider, there's always something to be grateful for.

When you look at your life with an attitude of gratitude, you'll suddenly find a new appreciation for each day. And when you appreciate each day for even the simplest of things, it's much easier to retain that positive attitude.

Chapter Seven

ARISE AND SHINE

Isaiah 60:1 New King James Version declares:

Arise, shine;
For your light has come!
And the glory of
the Lord is risen upon you.

Each morning is a new opportunity to enjoy your life and take another step towards achieving your dreams.

Yet so many people wake up and just go through the same old motions as they do every other day. They breathe. They eat and walk and talk. They work. They go home. They watch TV.

They do only what needs to be done to get them through their day until it's time to sleep again. And then they wake up and repeat the whole process again the next day.

When you wake up each morning, what's your first thought?

Do you dread getting out of bed and getting started? Do you groan at the thought of all the mundane chores you have to do throughout your day? Do you dread sitting in peak hour traffic to get to your boring job so you can deal with your awful colleagues yet again?

The Power of
POSITIVE AFFIRMATIONS

What if you woke up each morning and believed that each new dawn was a new opportunity to take another step towards a bright future?

Would that change how you acted throughout each day? Would your attitude be different if you knew that today was the start of something really BIG?

Before you get out of bed each morning, take a moment to focus on your thoughts. Build up your own mental image of how you want your life to look. Use those moments before you rise each day to imagine yourself living the happy, healthy, abundant life you really want.

Write down some simple affirmations that help you stay focused on what you want to achieve. Repeat those affirmations regularly.

Your daydreams are the first step to creating positive thoughts that turn into positive actions. Use them to your advantage.

NEVER GIVE UP

The main reason most people never achieve their dreams is because they give up.

Imagine if you had a bunch of keys and you're standing in front of a locked door. You might try five or six of those keys and give up. But if you'd persisted you would eventually find the right key to open that door.

The same analogy is true with almost everything you do.

Sure, it may take you a few attempts to gain any momentum. You may even figure out that you made some mistakes along the way.

What if you were climbing a mountain and you gave up because you just couldn't see the top? There might be clouds circling the peak of that mountain obscuring your vision, but it doesn't mean the top has vanished.

It's still there. It's just hidden from your view.

If you give up climbing and go home, you'll never know just how close you came to success.

Even if you can't see the end goal of your dreams or desires, don't give up aiming at them. The prize might be just another few steps beyond your vision, but it's right there just the same.

The point is, if you never give up you'll eventually find the right way to achieve the things you want in your life.

The easiest way to stay motivated and on track to achieving your dreams is to work on changing your thoughts. Believe it's possible.

If you can't find a way to believe in your current skill set, look for ways to learn new things that can help you achieve success. Ask questions of people around you who might be able to help you find the right solutions.

The key to reaching your goals is to persist. Trust that the goal is before you, even if you can't see it right now. As long as you're taking small, positive steps in the right direction you'll get there eventually.

Never give up.

Chapter Eight

CONCLUSION

Learning to adopt a positive attitude means you should be able to enjoy every aspect of your life right now without waiting for something big in your future. You don't need more money or more success to be happy.

In fact, you can be immensely happy right now with exactly what you have today.

Change your thoughts and focus on being grateful for what you've already achieved and the things you already have. Find ways to curb

those negative thoughts and turn them around into positive ones instead.

Each time you repeat those positive thoughts, they gain strength. They have the power to change your words.

When you speak positive, empowering words, you reinforce your thoughts, which make them even stronger again and the cycle gains momentum.

It's only when your thoughts and your words reach that point that your actions will start to follow. You'll find it easier to reach for opportunities you might otherwise have let pass you by. You'll deal with life's stresses more easily and you'll feel happier about even the little things that happen each day.

If you're serious about living a happy, healthy and abundant life, the key is to change your thoughts. Take control of those negative

thoughts and emotions and turn them around. Find affirmations that help you stick to a positive frame of mind, and then repeat them until you feel more confident about them.

Your thoughts really can change your life.

"The Lord bless you and keep you;
The Lord make His face shine upon you,
And be gracious to you;
The Lord lift up His countenance upon you,
And give you peace." - **Numbers 6:24-26** New King James Version.

God bless you!

Prayers, Decrees and Declarations based on the Word of God - Proclaim with boldness.

Jesus said, "It is the Spirit who gives life; the flesh profits nothing. The words that I speak to you are spirit, and they are life". **John 6:63** New King James Version.

Matthew 18:18 King James Version says:

"Verily I say unto you, Whatsoever ye shall bind on earth shall be bound in heaven: and whatsoever ye shall loose on earth shall be loosed in heaven."

Job 22:28 New American Standard Version tells us:

"You will also decree a thing, and it will be established for you;
And light will shine on your ways.

And then, **Ephesians 6:12** New King James Version says:

For we do not wrestle against flesh and blood, but against principalities, against powers, against the rulers of the darkness of this age, against spiritual hosts of wickedness in the heavenly places.

Now, let's look closer at **Ezekiel 37:1-10** New King James Version:

The hand of the Lord came upon me and brought me out in the Spirit of the Lord, and set me down in the midst of the valley; and it was full of bones. Then He caused me to pass by them all around, and behold, there were very many in the open valley; and indeed they were very dry. And He said to me, "Son of man, can these bones live?"

So I answered, "O Lord God, You know."

Again He said to me, "Prophesy to these bones, and say to them, 'O dry bones, hear the word of the Lord! Thus says the Lord God to these bones: "Surely I will cause breath to enter into you, and you shall live. I will put sinews on you and bring flesh upon you, cover you with skin and put breath in you; and you shall live. Then you shall know that I am the Lord."

So I prophesied as I was commanded; and as I prophesied, there was a noise, and suddenly a rattling; and the bones came together, bone to bone. Indeed, as I looked, the sinews and the flesh came upon them, and the skin covered them over; but there was no breath in them.

Also He said to me, "Prophesy to the breath, prophesy, son of man, and say to the breath, 'Thus says the Lord God: "Come from the four winds, O breath, and breathe on these slain, that they may live." So I prophesied as He

commanded me, and breath came into them, and they lived, and stood upon their feet, an exceedingly great army.

By the authority of Jesus Christ (The Anointed One), I decree and declare that:

- This week I shall experience a dramatic increase in favour, in the name of Jesus.
- This day, I shall attract necessary attention by the reason of God's favour upon my life, In the name of Jesus.

- The favour of God will go ahead of me and announce me before my arrival, in the name of Jesus.

- My destiny is decorated with favour, in the name of Jesus.

- I carry a global generational favour, in the name of Jesus.

- I am a child of generational favour, in the name of Jesus.

- A favoured man / woman is a mobile attraction therefore; I shall continually attract favour wherever I go, in the name of Jesus.

- I am prosperous because of the favour of God upon my life, in Jesus name.

- I have been transformed by the favour of God, in Jesus name.

- The favour of God will make things that labour cannot get to happen, in Jesus name.

- My name shall be mentioned for good because it carries a fragrance of favour.

- I shall experience a dimension of favour that distinguishes me and erase my struggles, in Jesus name.

- Mercy and favour shall locate me as I start my day, in Jesus name.

- The favour of God will protect me and my household, in Jesus name.
- I am walking in favour, in Jesus name.
- I shall stand strong in the place of prayer, in Jesus name.
- I shall not be found wanting in the place of prayer, in Jesus name.
- My altar of prayer will not fail, in Jesus name.
- Every attack on my prayer life, is cursed in Jesus name.
- My strength is renewed in the altar of prayer, in Jesus name.

The Power of
POSITIVE AFFIRMATIONS

- I receive the spirit of grace and supplication, in Jesus name.

- This day, people will use my career as a prayer point, in Jesus name.

- This day, people will use my business as a prayer point, in Jesus name.

- Longevity is my portion by the reason of my fasting and prayer, in Jesus name.

- My God is a prayer answering God.

- I am anointed for breakthrough in my prayer life, in Jesus name.

- Every prayer draining spirit is cast out, in Jesus name.

- Answers to my prayers shall be facilitated this day, in Jesus name.
- I am walking into fortune and prosperity, in Jesus name.
- I have been translated into the Kingdom of light, in Jesus name.
- I am a child of authority, in Jesus name.
- I am a child of honour, in Jesus name.
- I have a glorious future, in Jesus name.
- Impossibilities are delivered supernaturally, in Jesus name.
- Every of my heart's desires shall be delivered, in Jesus name.

- Every weapon of the devil is paralysed, in Jesus name.

- I am a blessed child, in Jesus name.

- I am for signs and wonders, in Jesus name.

- I am a winner, in Jesus name.

- I shall live to declare the works, glory and counsel of the Lord in the land of the living, in the name of Jesus Christ.

- Death has no power over me; therefore I shall not be subjected to death, in the name of Jesus Christ.

- Death is swallowed up in Jesus name.

- God has ransomed me from the power of the grave, therefore long life is my portion, in the name of Jesus Christ.

- Situations will not cloud my vision from seeing the clarity of God, in the name of Jesus Christ.

- Oppression of the devil is terminated, in the name of Jesus Christ.

- I have total health, in the name of Jesus Christ.

- Every assignment of the grave is destroyed, in the name of Jesus Christ.

- Every sentence of death is lifted up by the life in the Blood of Jesus.

The Power of
POSITIVE AFFIRMATIONS

- Every rod of the magician, enchanter, and necromancer is swallowed up by the reason of Calvary, in the name of Jesus Christ.

- The Blood of Jesus has set me free from sin and sorrow.

- I take dominion over ill health, in the name of Jesus Christ.

- My dominion is rooted in the power of God.

- The power of God is more than sufficient to heal me.

- The harassment of darkness in my life has come to an end by the arrival of light, in the name of Jesus Christ.

- I am operating in the realm of unquestionable dominion, in the name of Jesus Christ.
- I shall not be stranded at the cross road of life, in the name of Jesus Christ.
- My God shall work through me and with me, in the name of Jesus Christ.
- I am a child of vision.
- I can see the unveiling of God's divine plan in my life, in the name of Jesus Christ.
- My inheritance is guaranteed by the Holy Spirit.

- I am redeemed from every curse, enchantment and divination, in the name of Jesus Christ.

- I shall live a hurt free life and curse free existence, in the name of Jesus Christ.

- I curse whatever is trying to snatch life from me, in the name of Jesus Christ.

- My struggles are converted to breakthroughs by the reason of resurrection, in the name of Jesus Christ.

- The seed of poverty mentality is cursed, in Jesus name.

- I am going into greater heights, in Jesus name.

- I am scaling new heights, in Jesus name.

- The Lord is advancing me just as He advanced Moses and Aaron, in Jesus name.

- I refuse to accept stagnation, in Jesus name.

- Every chains of bondage is breaking down as my light breaks forth, in Jesus name.

- As my light breaks forth, no power or force shall dominate me, in Jesus name.

- My God is showing me great and mighty things as I call upon him, in Jesus name.

- Every arena of my life is perfect because the Bible says every good and perfect gift comes from God.

- I know my redeemer liveth, therefore nothing can steal my life nor my faith, in Jesus name.

- By faith, I am fully persuaded of the truth that my God reigneth above principalities and powers, not withstanding the prevailing circumstances.

- Heaven on earth is a reality for me by faith.

- I shall continue to engage in faith filled words in order to see prophesies of God fulfilled in my life, in Jesus name.

- I release the judgement of heaven upon every power that will not let me go, in Jesu' name.

- Every strongman that will not let me advance must go for my sake, in Jesus name.
- I am a mother of children, because God gives conception.
- My children shall be mighty and they shall sit on thrones in my lifetime, in Jesus name.
- Arise Oh Lord and let every snare of the fowler be caught in their own snare, in Jesus name.
- Lord arise and let everyone that has dug a pit for me fall into it, in the name of Jesus.
- King of glory, arise and let every gate be lifted.

- Everyone troubling my destiny, family, career and marital destiny be cut down, in Jesus name.

- I decree that every wicked machination be cut down, in Jesus name.

- Anyone coming against me from the house of wickedness shall be cut off, in Jesus name.

- God's plans and purpose for my life will manifest in due times and season, in Jesus name.

- The enemy will not abort the plans and purpose of God in my life, in Jesus name.

- I will continue to celebrate the Word of God through praise.

- As I praise God, let vengeance fall upon the camp of my enemies.

- Supernatural turnaround is my portion as I praise God.

- My mouth shall continue to praise God, because praise is a fountain of wonders.

- I use praise as a weapon to war against every demonic manipulations and human resistance to my rising.

- Every written promise of God for my life shall be turned into a testimony as I praise my God.

The Power of
POSITIVE AFFIRMATIONS

- All round triumph is my portion by the reason of God's presence in my life, in Jesus name.

- The Blood of Jesus will continue to speak in my life.

- Every demonic influence around my children are destroyed, in Jesus name.

- Every satanic voice of confusion is silenced, in Jesus name.

- Every mountain must shift because I carry the presence of God.

- Every gate must open because I carry the presence of God.

- I am covered by the Blood of Jesus.

- My Family is covered by the Blood of Jesus.

- He is God and will always be God.

- Breakthrough shall be my identity, in Jesus name.

- Thank you mighty God.

- What I see determines my change – I see greatness, divine order of favour, recommendation, intervention, health, multiplication and power, in Jesus name.

- I shall see great and mighty things by the power of God.

- Unspeakable joy is my portion.

- Peace that passes all understanding is my portion, in Jesus name.

The Power of
POSITIVE AFFIRMATIONS

- I shall enjoy divine supply, in Jesus name.

- This day, my eyes shall see the goodness of God.

- God is crushing both the executer and motivator of evil in my life, in Jesus name.

- The wickedness of the wicked shall not manifest in my life, in Jesus name.

- I decree the falling of every gathering with satanic wicked intention, in Jesus name.

- Longevity and vitality is my portion, in Jesus name.

- I shall not fail

- I shall not fall

- This day I shall flow in divine wisdom.

The Power of
POSITIVE AFFIRMATIONS

- Only goodness and mercy shall follow me all through this year, in Jesus name.
- My God will daily load me with benefits, in Jesus name.
- This is my season of exploits, in Jesus name.
- I will speak of the Glory of God.
- This year, I will enjoy the best of God.
- I am a chosen generation call forth to show His excellence.
- I am successful.
- I am prosperous.
- God will give me a notable miracle.
- My season of dryness is finally over.
- All my years, I will know no lack.

- I shall command supernatural abundance, in Jesus name.
- I shall live a pain free life, in Jesus name.
- A life full of vitality is my portion, in Jesus name.
- The joy of the Lord is my strength.
- I shall hold my peace because God is fighting my battle.
- I overcome the spirit of fear with the Word of God.
- I shall enjoy forceful advancement, in Jesus name.
- I shall not engage in a purposeless living, in Jesus name.

The Power of
POSITIVE AFFIRMATIONS

- I shall attain great heights, in Jesus name.

- I shall not be slothful.

- My gifting shall not be wasted, in Jesus name.

- I am designed by God to stand out, separated and elevated.

- I declare my liberty and freedom, in the name of Jesus.

- God is my advantage.

- The Holy Spirit is my helper.

- The Lord is my light and my salvation.

- Jesus has set me free.

- I come against every spirit of bondage.

The Power of
POSITIVE AFFIRMATIONS

- I come against every lying spirit, in Jesus name.

- I bind every spirit of whoredom, in Jesus name.

- My life shall be noted for reigning, in Jesus name.

- My generation shall be blessed, in Jesus name.

- Upon mount Zion there shall be deliverance.

- I shall possess my possession, in Jesus name.

- The peace that passeth all understanding is my portion, in Jesus name.

- My God will empower me with the grace for righteousness.
- My prayer shall not be hindered, in Jesus name.
- My God will restore health unto me, in the mighty name of Jesus.
- I am redeemed to shine, in the mighty name of Jesus.
- I am redeemed to be exempted from every financial holocaust, in the mighty name of Jesus.
- I shall be lifted in my finances, in Jesus name.

- An end has come to every financial crisis in my life, in Jesus name.

- I will never be grounded, in Jesus name.

- God will turn me and my household to a financial surprise, in the mighty name of Jesus.

- I shall be lifted in my place of work, in Jesus name.

- I shall be lifted in my academics, in Jesus name.

- My generation after me will not know lack, in the mighty name of Jesus.

- I am ordained for financial fortune as a seed of Abraham.

- My era of financial fortune is finally here.

- Our marital destiny is blessed therefore every attendee of our wedding shall favour and honour us.

- My Heavenly Father, I thank you for another wonderful time in your presence.

- I shall be fruitful and I shall multiply according to the Word of God. Gen1:28.

- I speak to every coven, grove and principalities in my arena. I decree that their operation comes to an end because the earth is the Lords and the fullness thereof. Ps24:1

- God of protection and preservation, arise and protect my family and I from being consumed in the valley of the shadow of death according to your Word in Psalm 23:4

- I shall be first among equals and there shall be lifting up for me always, in Jesus name.

- I claim fresh opportunities this day, in Jesus name.

- King of glory I thank you for the blessing of sleeping and waking up.

- King of glory, I thank you for the breath of life in me.

- I shall not be found wanting in the things of the Kingdom, in Jesus name.

- This day I receive fresh business ideas, in Jesus name.

- Father, let Malachi3:10 find speedy expression in my life as I obey you with my tithe and offering, in Jesus name.

- Lord I declare that you shall do a new thing in my life and I shall be happily married to the glory of God and the shame of the devil, in Jesus name.

- My health is restored. My body and bones are refreshed as I eat the Word of God, just as Jeremiah declared.

- I decree and declare that every arena of my life shall experience the peace and glory of God, in Jesus name.

- I prophesy that this week honour shall be my experience, in the name of Jesus.

- I prophesy that this week, there shall be a dramatic increase of favour.

- Every counsel of Ahithophel shall be turned into foolishness, in Jesus name.

- Every bad news is converted to good news, in Jesus name.

- Any of my belonging still withheld by the forces of darkness is released, in Jesus name.

- God will prepare my way with favour.

- Every yoke of delay is broken, in Jesus name.

- My testimony shall be a pointer to others of God's hand at work in my life, in Jesus name.

- I am redeemed to command supernatural breakthrough, in Jesus name.

- Every academic reproach is rolled away, in Jesus name.

- I shall not be put to shame in Jesus name.

- My righteousness shall shine like the brightness of the day, in Jesus name.

- Every hindrance, frustration and limitation is broken, in Jesus name.

- It is of a truth that what I speak determines what I see; therefore, I declare that I shall arrive at my destination, in Jesus name.

- I decree that the unquenchable fire of God burns anything contrary to the Word of God in my life, in Jesus name.

- Every barrier is broken by the authority of Jesus.

- I decree and declare that there shall be no more delay and every yoke is broken by the power of the Holy Ghost.

- Merciful Father, I bless your Holy name for the dawning of a new day and the reward of life.

Thank you for your Word in Jesus name. Amen.

Check Out Other Books:

- In The **Pursuit of Wisdom**: The Principal Thing

- Investing in **Gold and Silver** Bullion - The Ultimate Safe Haven Investments

- **Nigerian Stock Market Investment**: 2 Books with Bonus Content

- The **Dividend Millionaire**: Investing for Income and Winning in the Stock Market

- Economic Crisis: Surviving Global Currency Collapse - Safeguard Your **Financial Future with Silver and Gold**

- **Passionate about Stock Investing**: The Quick Guide to Investing in the Stock Market

- Guide to Investing in the Nigerian Stock Market

- **Building Wealth with** Dividend Stocks in the **Nigerian Stock Market** (Dividends - Stocks Secret Weapon)

- Beginners Basic Guide to Investing in Gold and Silver Boxed Set

- Beginners Basic Guide to Stock Market Investment Boxed Set

- **Precious Metals Investing** For Beginners: The Quick Guide to Platinum and Palladium

- **Bitcoin and Digital Currency** for Beginners: **The Basic Little Guide**

- **Child Millionaire**: Stock Market Investing for Beginners - How to Build Wealth the Smart Way for Your Child

- **Christian Living: 2 Books with Bonus Content**

- Beginners Quick Guide to Passive Income: Learn **Proven Ways to Earn Extra Income** in the Cyber World

- **Taming the Tongue: The Power of Spoken Words**

If you would like to share this book with another person, please purchase an additional copy for each recipient. Thank you for respecting the hard work of this author.

CPSIA information can be obtained
at www.ICGtesting.com
Printed in the USA
LVOW13s1305010317
525803LV00017B/484/P